LEARNING TO LIVE, LEARNING TO LOVE

"The Present World is full of so much darkness, that we need strong reminders that there is light, and reason for hope as well because we have ourselves. LEARNING TO LIVE, LEARNING TO LOVE is such a reminder."

— *Virginia Satir*
PEOPLE MAKING

LEARNING TO LIVE, LEARNING TO LOVE

By
Joanne Haynes-Klassen

Jalmar Press
Rolling Hills Estates, California

Published by Jalmar Press
45 Hitching Post Drive, Building 2
Rolling Hills Estates, California 90274

Production Coordinator: Janet Lovelady
Cover: Gerald Loewen & Willene Moffat-Cox
Cover Photo: Russ Mead
Artwork: Willene Moffat-Cox & Judy Ferguson

Library of Congress Catalog Card Number: 83-080076
Printed in the United States of America
ISBN: 0-915190-38-9

**Library of Congress Cataloging in Publication
Data**

Haynes-Klassen, Joanne.
    Learning to live, learning to love.

    1. Love—Psychological aspects. 2. Success.
I. Title.
BF575.L8H37   1985   158'.1   84-742
ISBN 0-915190-38-9 (pbk.)

THIS BOOK IS DEDICATED TO my children, Tiffany and Anna Haynes, Mike, Steven and Ted Klassen, Jr. — and to the precious child within each person.

ACKNOWLEDGMENTS

To the many people who have contributed to the heart of this book, I'd like to say thank you.

To those from whom I received the gift of love and acceptance, Don and Peg Hindal, my parents.

To Ted Klassen, my husband, with whom I have discovered the special wonder of intimate love: the power of trust, patience and forgiveness.

To Nina Colwill, master of the art of friendship, for endless support and understanding.

To Stan Woolhams who, as a professional, taught me the power of loving concern in changing lives — even in one hour.

To Beverly (her middle name is encouragement) Suek, who steadfastly believes in people.

To Diane Krahn whose vibrant joy at the accomplishments of others and unfailing faith have often saved me from despair.

To Blair Fraser and Carol Kemp for their contributions.

To Suzanne Mikesell, Jalmar Editor, whose loving questioning and guidance moved me to deeper levels of understanding and clarity.

To the many people in my workshops who have shared with me their struggles and joys in learning to live, learning to love. You have shared a part of your journey with me — this is really **your** book.

I have experienced the loving ways of the following people and through their example I have found the courage and inspiration to share what I believe:

Mother Teresa of Calcutta, Dru Scott, Leo Buscaglia, Clark Moustakas, Muriel James, Carl Rogers and John Powell.

I am especially grateful to the author of life, from whom **all** blessings flow.

PREFACE

Important things are often quite simple.

The important ideas in this book are presented in simple language.

My hope is that you will share these ideas with your special people — children, teenagers and adults.

This book is for friends, husbands and wives, parents and children and grandparents.

It is for teachers and students, it is for home, school, office, clinic, church and library.

Most of all — this book is for

YOU.

Simple things are not necessarily easy. If you are finding that learning to live and learning to love are at times difficult, you are in good company. People everywhere are finding it a tough challenge — including me.

Enjoy!

Joanne Haynes-Klassen

CONTENTS

INTRODUCTION

This is a book about
YOU.

It is a book about
EVERYONE.

Hi. I'm Everyone. I am a symbol for **ALL** people everywhere.

You will see me change into many kinds of people.

**Perhaps some of them will remind you of
yourself and people you know.**

5

This book is about learning to give and receive love. In order to give to others and to life, **we must begin by learning to love and accept ourselves.** We will be talking about learning to love and accept:

Ourselves

Others

and
Life

Part 1

Looking Inside

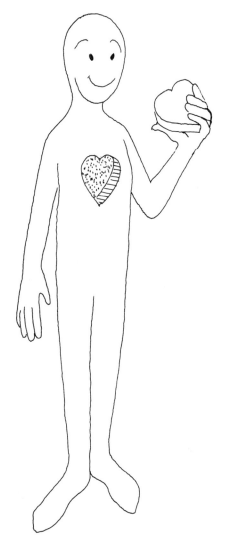

People are born with a special place inside.
It is designed to be filled with love and
acceptance.

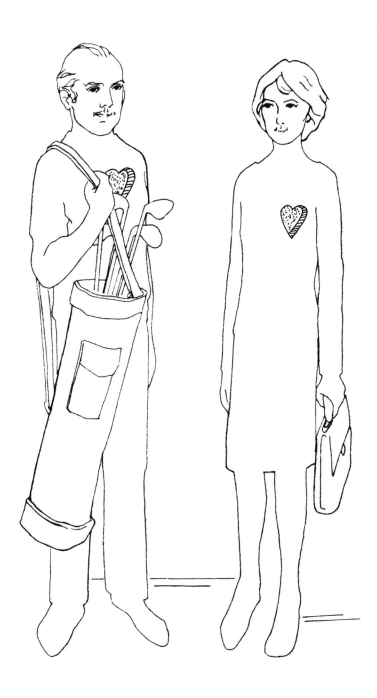

This is the way people are made. Nothing else can fill the place of love.

It may be hard to understand this because no
one tells us this secret when we are born.

No instruction book telling how we operate is given to us at birth.

We couldn't read it anyway!

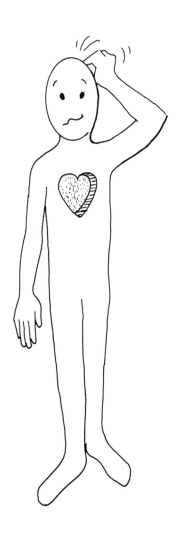

What is **love?**
What is **acceptance?**

People talk about love in many ways.
"I love my cat."
"I love ice cream."
"I love rainy days."
"I love you."

In this book, love means valuing the specialness of each person without judging him or her.

By ACCEPTANCE we mean respecting the way a person is without wanting him or her to be different to please us.

Part 2

Mistakes About Our Emptiness

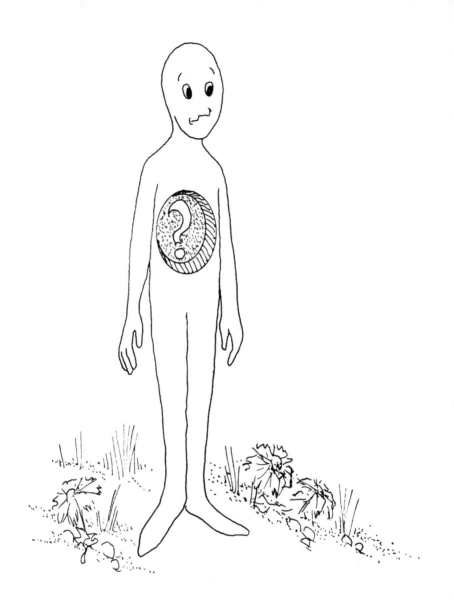

Some people don't understand their need for love and acceptance. They feel empty inside but they don't know why.

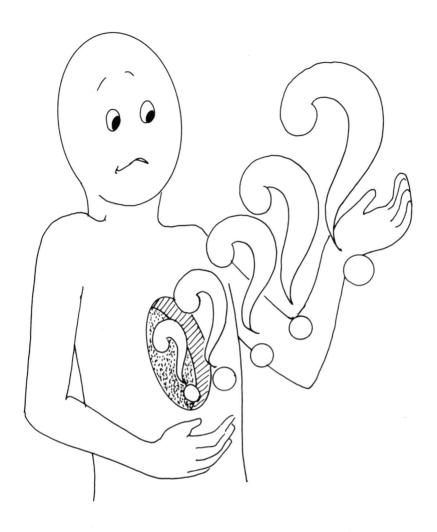

Sometimes they get mixed-up about how to fill
this emptiness. When they try to fill it with
things other than love and acceptance, the
empty feeling only grows bigger.

Some people try to fill the emptiness inside
with food. They overeat on snacks and
sweets.

But they feel emptier and emptier and less good about themselves. They also look chubby, so you can tell they still need love and acceptance.

Some people try to fill this place with alcohol
(also known as booze). They drink too much
wine or whiskey or beer.

20

But they feel emptier and emptier and less good about themselves. They also smell of booze and don't talk or act the same as usual, so you can tell they still need love and acceptance.

Some people try to fill their emptiness by taking drugs. They take pills or other types of drugs.

But they feel emptier and emptier and less good about themselves. They also may act dazed or half asleep, so you can tell they still need love and acceptance.

Some people try to fill the empty space inside of them with things. They buy lots of stuff they don't need. (They may even buy things for you.)

But they feel emptier and emptier and less good about themselves. They also are surrounded by things, and talk about money, so you can tell they still need love and acceptance.

Some people try to fill the emptiness inside of them with sex. They spend time sleeping with or making love with lots of different people.

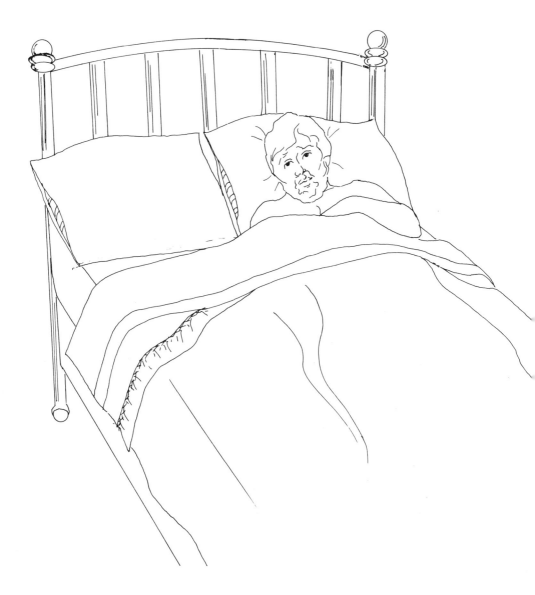

But they feel emptier and emptier and less
good about themselves. They also try to look
sexy and may wear tight clothes and
make-up or un-buttoned shirts, so you can
tell they still need love and acceptance.

Some people try to fill the emptiness by doing many things for others and hoping for their approval in return.

But they feel emptier and emptier and less
good about themselves. They may keep
trying to do things for you, so you can tell
they still need love and acceptance.

Some people try to fill the empty place inside of them with work. They rush to meetings, committees and clubs. They are always very busy.

But they feel emptier and even less good
about themselves. They also look often at
their watches or schedules and don't seem to
relax with you, so you can tell they still need
love and acceptance.

Some people do two or three or even four of these things to try to fill the emptiness inside them. But people usually specialize in one way.

The need for love is buried behind

eating too much,

drinking too much,

taking drugs,

buying things,

casual sex,

pleasing others

or overwork.

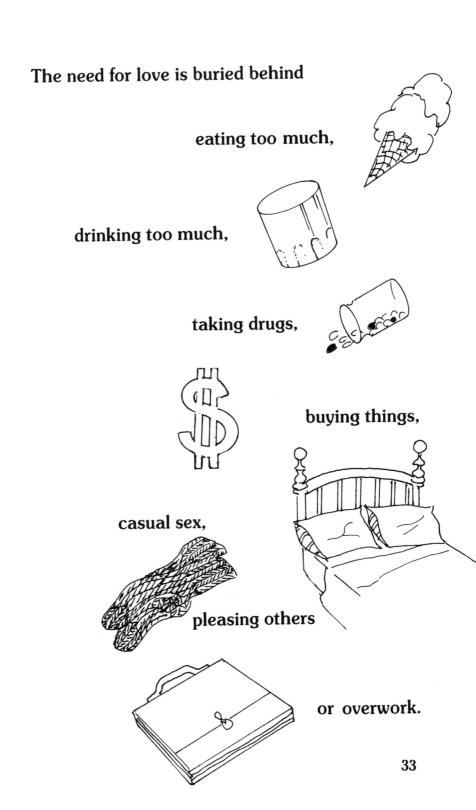

When people do such things over and over
again we call the pattern an **ADDICTION**.
People with addictions feel alone and out of
control.

What do all these ways of dealing with
emptiness have in common? That's right.
THEY DON'T WORK!

Most people suspect this. They get very tired
from doing things that don't work — things
that leave them feeling less and less good
about themselves. They feel angry or sad or
hurt or scared or confused or exhausted.
They seem to be stuck. They don't know what
to do.

Can you imagine how much time and energy
people would have for the business of good
living and loving if they understood their
need for love?

What can we do to change these patterns?

Part 3

Learning to Love Yourself

A first step in learning to live, learning to love is to recognize that in one way you are like all people everywhere.

You need love and acceptance in order to feel whole.

Nothing will grow well unless it gets the things it needs.

Plants need light.

Animals need food.

People need many more things.

We need to feel special and to be loved and accepted for who we are.

You have as much right to what you need as
other living things — plants, animals or people.

Whether you accept this idea or not, it is true.
You are no different from any other person in
needing to be loved. You deserve love just as
much as anyone anywhere.

Understanding this is an important part of
accepting yourself. Your needs are part of
you. This is especially true of your need to be
loved.

No, not when you change or improve, but
RIGHT NOW. Just as you are this minute.
YOU ARE LOVEABLE.

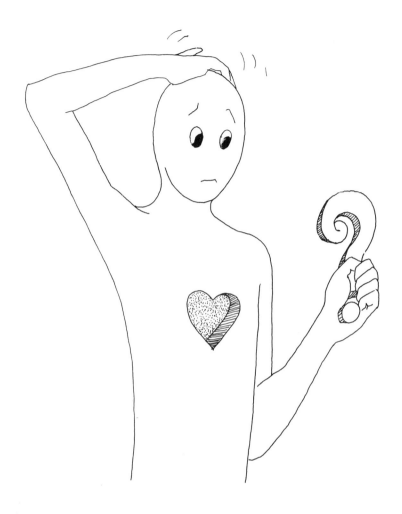

Who is the best person to begin loving and accepting you right now? Here is a clue: this person is close at hand and available. This person understands all your needs, hopes and fears.

You guessed it: it's **Y O U**. What are you
waiting for?

YOU ARE A SPECIAL, VALUABLE, WONDERFUL, UNIQUE PERSON.

Never since the beginning of time has there been another person exactly like you. No one can do and think and feel quite as you do.

Because of who you are it makes sense for you to make friends with yourself, to be on friendly terms with you. What will that take?

Let's begin with **PATIENCE.**

No one is perfect. Loving means being easy
with yourself even in your imperfection. You
are perfectly you, and that is as perfect as you
need to be right now.

Loving and accepting yourself means
choosing to express yourself in ways that are
just right for you.

Yes, you will let yourself **D**
O
W
N sometimes.
Then it is especially important to be your own
good friend.

How about forgiveness? You may be
ashamed of something you have done. Love
means forgiveness. Begin now to really
accept yourself by forgiving anything you did
"wrong" in the past.

Perhaps there is something you wish you
had not done or said. Perhaps there is
something you wish you **had** done or said.
Can you correct any of these things now?
Perhaps you can, and perhaps you will. If not,
let go of these things and make some room
for self-acceptance.

54

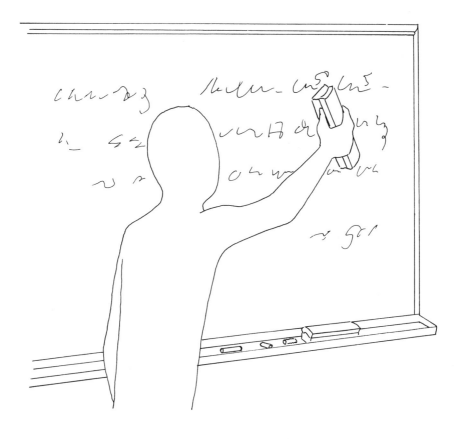

In your mind, picture a blackboard with all the "wrongs" you have done to yourself and to others written on it. Now walk up to it and begin to erase the board until it is clear and fresh.

As you do this, feel your self-forgiveness. You
may want to apologize by saying "I'm sorry"
as you let go and move ahead.

Loving yourself means recognizing your needs
and responding to them in a positive way.
You may find that as you value yourself more
you will want to be with people who are
important to you. You may choose to avoid
people who treat you as if your needs are
not important.

You can choose to stay away from such
people without judging them or you as "bad".
Loving yourself means knowing and doing
what is right for you, what is good for your
growth. It means increasing the number of
things that you do that are growthful for you.

You can trust yourself to make good choices.
Taking time to be aware of what is really best
for you is another way of loving yourself.
Sometimes you will make mistakes. That's
natural. You can learn something from each
mistake. Trust yourself. You are learning
and growing.

Loving yourself does **not** mean running away
from difficulties. It means facing them
honestly with respect for yourself and others.

When we do not love ourselves we sometimes
seek love by trying to please others. This
doesn't work. People who approach love this
way often feel under pressure or let down.
They get tired from trying so hard to measure
up to others' expectations. They end up
resenting the person they want to please.

With good loving there is pleasure in the
process of giving, and there is pleasure
afterward because love was given freely
rather than because it was expected.

When we love ourselves we have an abundance of love to share with others. We do not fear their expectations. We give freely what we choose to give — what is right for us. We find that we can love more than we ever expected. We can love a person for a moment, or an hour or a lifetime.

Loving in this way allows for growth without demanding from others or taking anything away from ourselves.

PART 4

Big and Small Matters

As we grow, we learn to do many new things.
We grow bigger, stronger and more capable
and sure of ourselves. But no matter how big
or strong or capable we grow to be, we
always have within a part that feels small
and unsure.

66

We all have this small part as well as the strong, assured part. We bring both along when meeting other people.

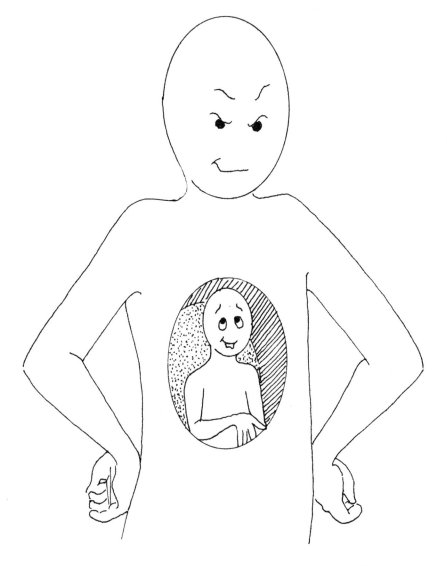

We may not like the small, unsure part of
ourselves. We may be afraid that others will
not like this part, either. We try to keep it a
secret by acting **big** and confident. That's
why it's often difficult to tell from the outside
what someone's feeling inside.

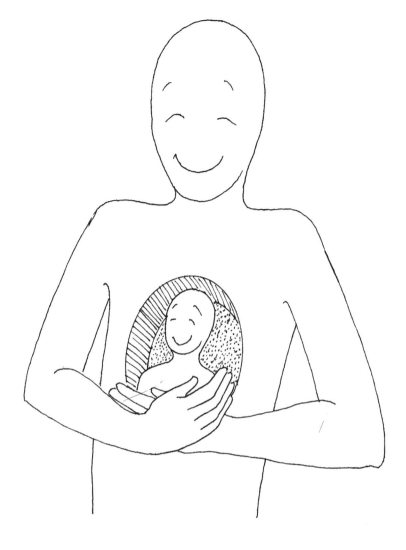

Yet the small part within the larger person we
are becoming is an important part of us.
Being grown-up doesn't mean we no longer
have a small person inside. As we grow, we
may learn more ways to respect and take
care of our small self. We may learn that it is
all right to let others know **all** of who we are.

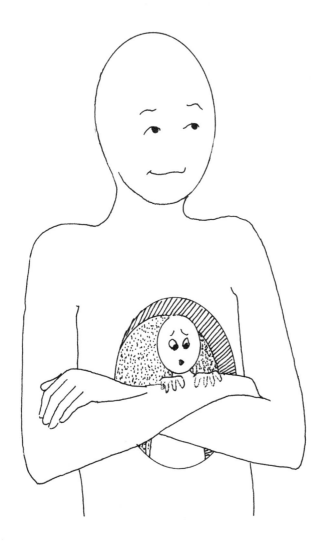

We may be able to **stop pretending** we are just the **BIG** part that others can see. When we let others see and know us, they may be able to share all of who they are with us. This is a special kind of love and acceptance that brings people closer together.

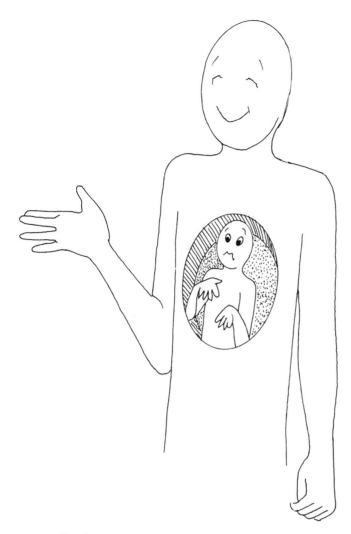

Only you can decide who will share your
thoughts and feelings. You may feel
frightened at first — especially if you have
tried for a long time to appear strong.

Remember, self-love means valuing all parts
of yourself. You can open new doors to loving
by honestly sharing your fears and
uncertainties along with your strengths.

PART 5

Treasure and Trash

Let's look at two kinds of ideas we have about
ourselves. **TREASURE** ideas are about what
is good, valuable, likable or loveable about us.

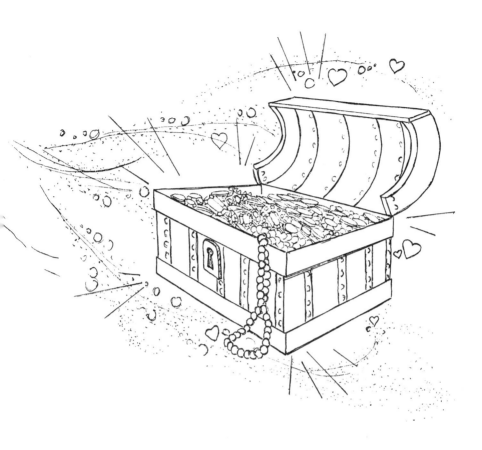

These ideas are like our own inner treasure chest of riches and jewels. Thinking about our good qualities, our strengths, talents and gifts makes us feel special and important.

We have other ideas about ourselves that are
not very positive. These ideas are about what
we think is wrong with us, our "bad"
qualities. We are ashamed of these "faults."
We wish we could cover them up or throw
them away so others wouldn't regard us as
worthless. These are **TRASH** ideas — they
make us feel bad.

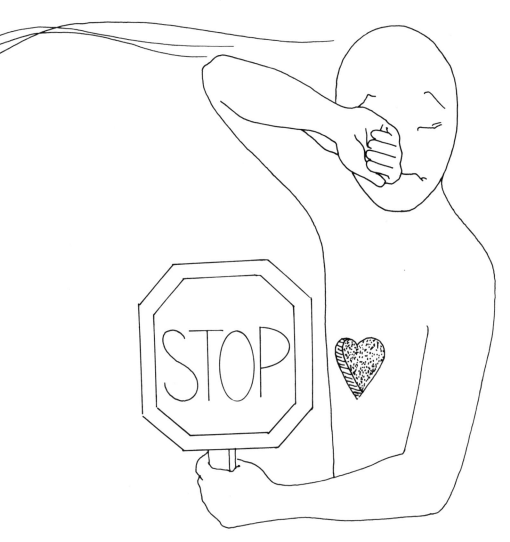

Make it a habit to develop your **TREASURE** ideas and thoughts about yourself. When you begin to think trash thoughts **STOP**. Begin to search for **treasure. YOU ALONE CHOOSE YOUR THOUGHTS.**

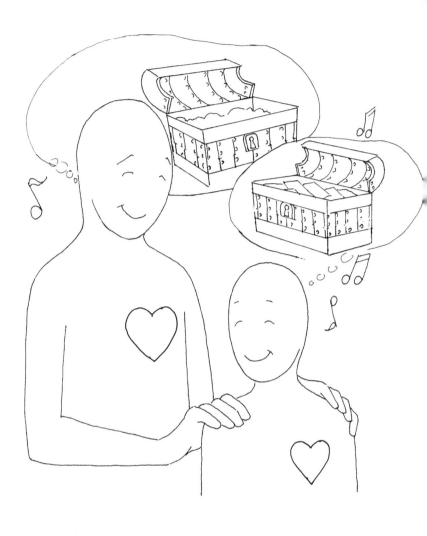

Your treasures are different from those of anyone else. Each person likes to have his or her treasures recognized. From the oldest to the youngest — hearing about our good qualities is music to our ears.

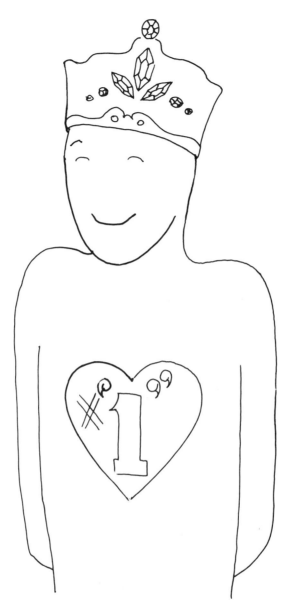

The truth is that **you are WONDERFUL just because you are you,** not because of what you can do or what you have or how you look or act. You are learning more and more each day about how to be fully yourself — unique and special. You are a one-of-a-kind original!

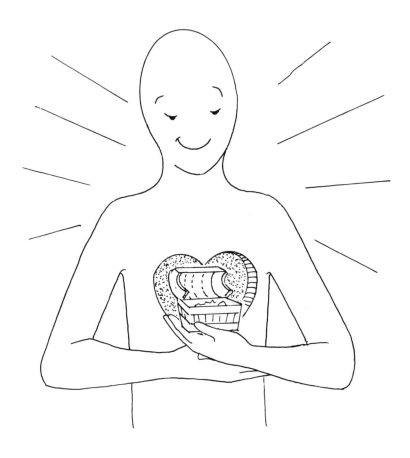

Even if no one else notices your specialness, it
is still yours. You can recognize it. Take time
to enjoy being you. There will be times when
you are alone. Recognizing your treasures is
especially important at these times. Alone
times can be perfect for discovering new
things to value about yourself.

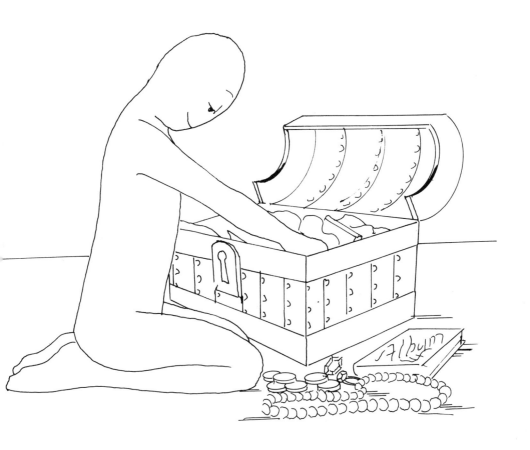

Begin now to sharpen your treasure-hunting
skills. Start by looking for your treasures.
What is good and special about you?
There are so many things. Identify at least
one or two right now. What are they?

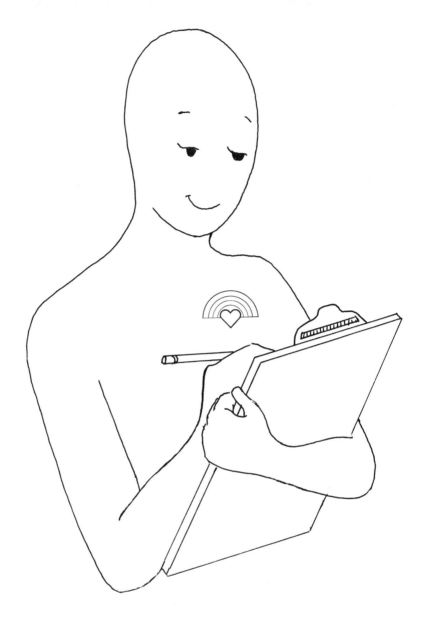

When stores count all the goods they have on hand, they call it "taking inventory." Whether you are young, old or in-between, taking inventory of your good qualities is a way to grow more loving. Write down your inventory in a special place. Keep adding to your inventory of personal strengths as you become aware of them.

At one time, a woman I know did not feel
comfortable writing down a single good thing
about herself. She felt shy and embarrassed.
She has grown in her ability to love herself
and others. Now she has a notebook with
many pages filled. (I know. I am that woman.)

Taking a personal inventory is easy once you
get started. You will come to know and love
yourself more fully. You will become more
open to knowing and loving others.

Maybe you have a collection of something you enjoy saving. Some people like to save stamps or coins or records. People collect all kinds of things. **The most valuable collection you can ever own is a collection of positive thoughts about your personal worth.**

No one can take away your collection of
good, kind, gentle thoughts about yourself as
long as you choose to keep it — no matter
what happens! You can add to your collection
every day. It costs you nothing and will make
you richer in countless ways.

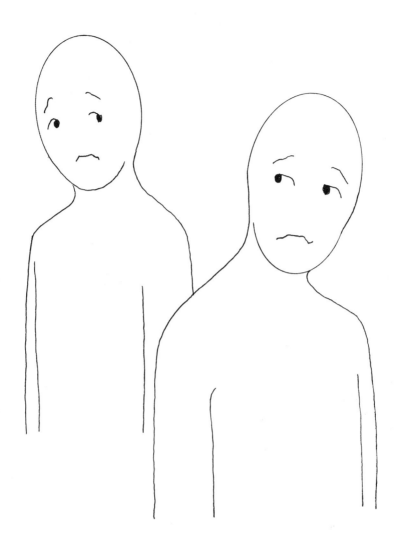

BE CAREFUL — people who don't think about their own treasures usually are not too good at seeing those in others. Being around this type of person is disappointing. Don't let it be **you.**

Learning to live, learning to love means being generous with the good we see in ourselves and others. It means being stingy about the not-so-good things we see. Always give yourself and others another chance. Our "trash" usually isn't what we think it is. We probably goofed in labelling it!

Things change and so do people. Remember, garbage is put into the garden and over time becomes compost — a terrific fertilizer that helps new plants grow. Transform your garbage thoughts as a way of helping yourself grow.

Caring about how others see us and what
they think of us is natural. But their opinions
of us are not as important as our own. No
matter what others see in us or how they
treat us, we can decide to greet ourselves
with the eyes of love and acceptance.

90

Only you can decide to throw out your trash
ideas. You **can** turn your attention to your
personal treasures and enjoy being who you
are. As you learn to do this you are learning
to love yourself better and more fully.
That is wonderful! 91

You may notice an interesting thing
beginning to happen. You are getting better
and better at noticing the treasure parts of
others and the world around you. You are
focusing more and more on the goodness
around you as you discover more of the
goodness within yourself.

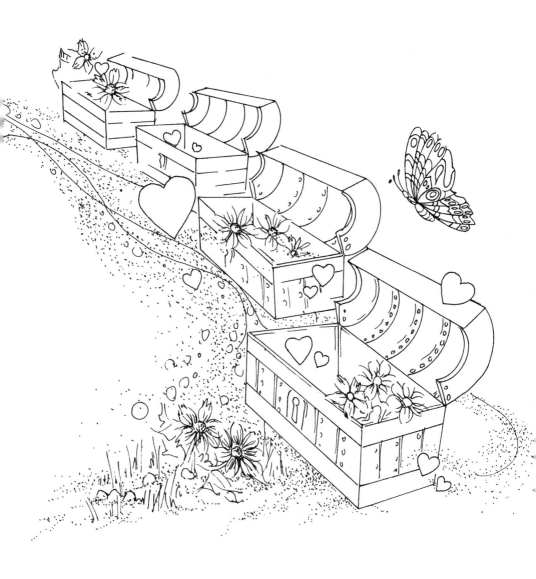

At the same time you notice less and less
trash in all those places. **Your ideas are
changing — along with them your
feelings will change, too.**

Doesn't it make sense to look within yourself to find ways of feeling whole? Looking within sure beats using food and alcohol and drugs and sex and money and overwork. **The choice is yours.** You are becoming more fully alive as you tune into yourself, **right now!**

PART 6

Learning to Love Others

As you learn to love and accept yourself just the way you are right now, you are learning some important lessons that will help you in loving others.

Learning to love many other people is
important to you. Although you may choose
to share certain types of love with only one
person, you have much more love to give
than one person could ever hold. One-to-one
relationships cannot replace the need for self
love or the need to be loving toward
many people.

If you depend on only a few people to give
love to and receive love from, you may find
lots of disappointment, conflict and
loneliness. These come not from loving too
much, but from holding back on the flow of
love that occurs naturally between people.

There are many different ways of loving others. As you grow, you will discover additional ways. Think about the many ways you are able to share love.

Here are a few:

— a letter or phone call to someone far away

— a smile for a stranger

— a supportive arm, a comforting hug

— letting someone know what you need or want

— understanding the special needs of a group of people who are different from you.

What are some of your favorite ways of showing love? You couldn't possible give all your love to one or two or ten people in your lifetime.

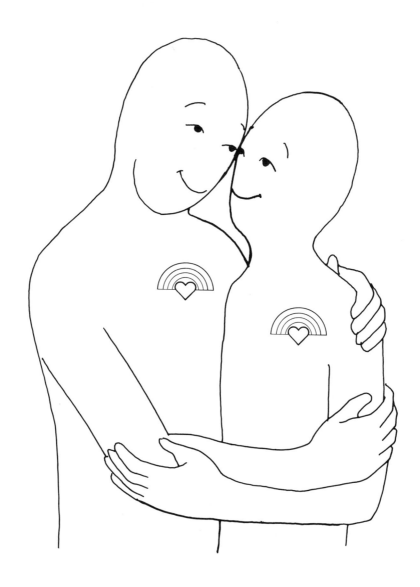

There are special people with whom you will
want to develop **L A R G E** WAYS OF
LOVING. When two people decide to share
much of themselves with one another in
closeness and love, this is something
wonderful. People sometimes call this an
"intimate relationship."

Intimacy can occur between any two caring
people: parent and child, sisters and brothers,
friends, husband and wife. The possibilities
are endless.

Loving others in an ongoing intimate
relationship requires some special skills. Let's
look at some of them.

Loving others means reaching out to them. It
means letting them know who you really are,
not just who you'd like to be. It means
accepting them for who they are, not just
who you'd like them to be. This is true for
new friends, old friends, family — parents and
children — and just about everyone else.

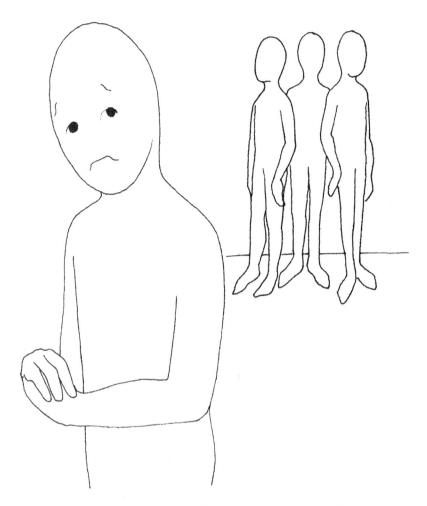

Letting others get to know us may not be
easy. We are afraid they may not like who we
are and will push us away or "reject" us. This
risk is always a part of loving and living
with others.

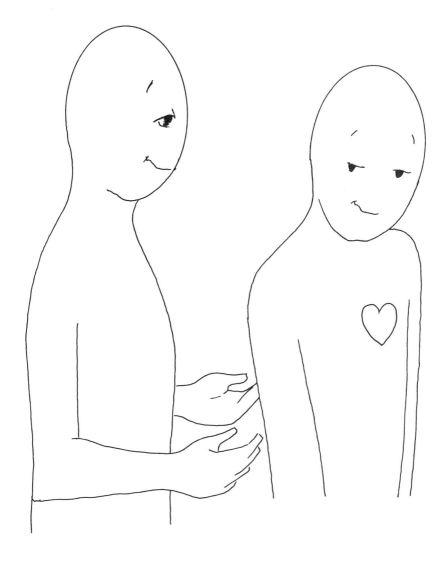

If you want love to grow between yourself and another person, there is no other way: you must risk being hurt and disappointed over and over again. There is no "safe" way to truly share love with others. You must let them know you.

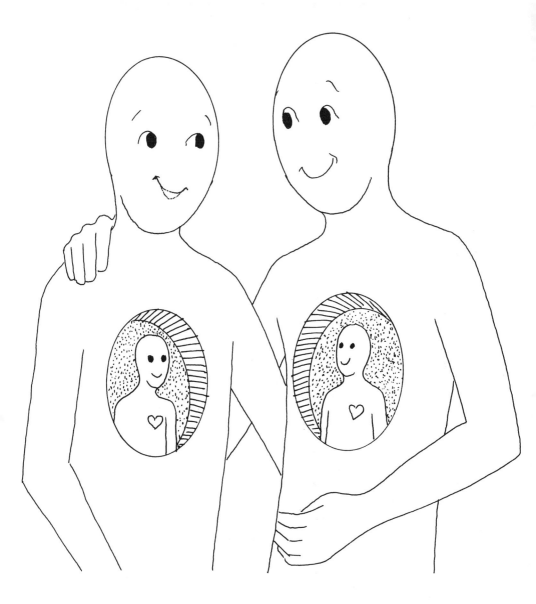

You must be determined to get to know the
other person. Each of you must get to know
the big and small parts of the other. Sharing
of this kind takes time and commitment. It's
easy to give up and stop loving when there
are difficulties between you. But if you want
the kind of love that is nurturing to both, you
must face even this challenge in loving.

We can see that loving others requires the same things as loving ourselves:

— being patient with change and imperfection

— being a friend, not letting go when you are let down

— forgiving

— trusting, even when mistakes are made and more . . .

Learning to love others also means **sharing.**
Sharing is exchanging:

— ideas and thoughts

— needs and feelings

— hopes and dreams

— beliefs and values

— time and things

You can share touch and contact, honesty
and privacy, silliness and seriousness,
laughter and tears, fun and hard work,
closeness and distance, giving and being
given to.

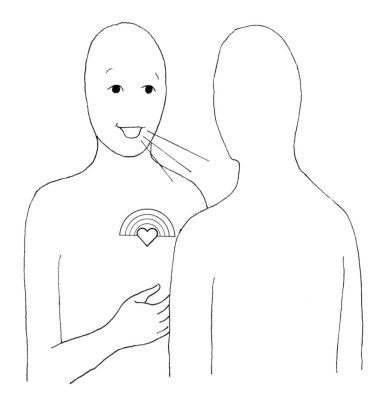

Sharing also involves talking and looking and listening and asking. Telling the other person what you think and feel about him or her is called "**feedback**."

Being good at loving means being good at giving feedback. You know how important it is for you to receive the feedback of others. Remember that they also need and want your feedback. Some people say "actions speak louder than words." Matching honest actions with words that express what we're thinking and feeling is powerful feedback.

Giving and receiving feedback is called
COMMUNICATION.
Communication is essential to loving
relationships.

Telling someone "I love you" is important
feedback.

Don't save it up! Could you give that
feedback to someone right now? Can you
visit, call or write to someone today to let
them know about your love? **Will you do it?**

Not all people with whom you want a loving
relationship will respond as you hope. Even
parents, children and dear friends and family
sometimes are unable to give you love in the
way you need it. Thank goodness there are
many, many people who will love you as you
risk reaching out, letting them know you and
getting to know them. Love can be found in
surprising places. Keep looking!

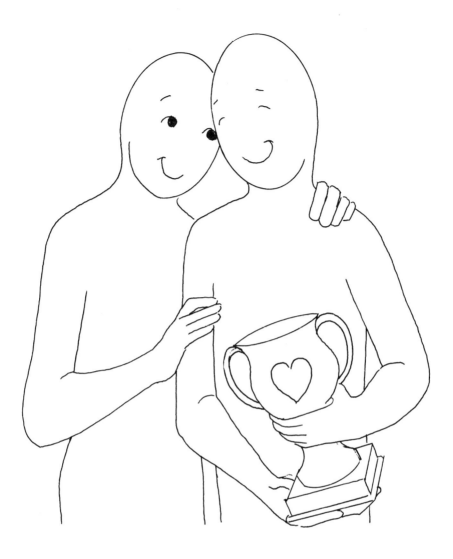

Learning to share love with another person
may be the hardest job you will face in your
life. But the reward will be worth all the effort.

In the past you have put lots of effort into other things that were very important to you. Learning to walk, talk, read, ride a bicycle and many other things are done when you are ready. Are you ready to learn to live and love more fully? **You** have what it takes.

PART 7

Learning to Love Life

We are connected with all of life. If we feel separated from other living things, we will feel alone. Making a loving connection with the world is a third important part of learning to live, learning to love.

As you grow, you will find many fun ways to give to and receive from life. Your ways may not have quite the same meaning for others as they do for you. You will discover some ways of enjoying life on your own and some with other people.

119

What do you appreciate in nature? Close your eyes right now. Can you hear any of these natural sounds:

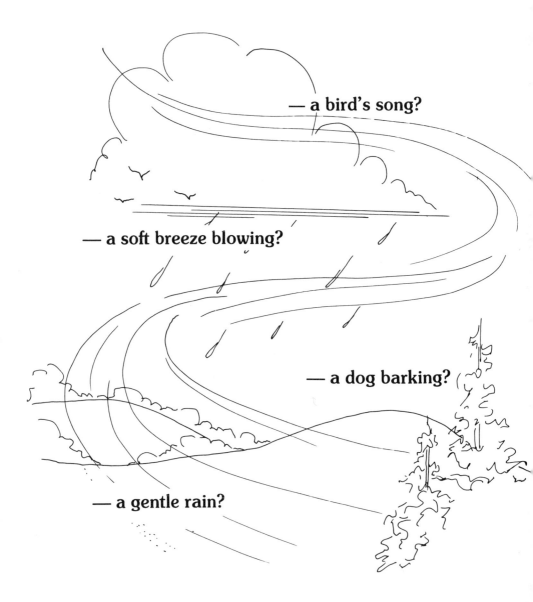

— a bird's song?

— a soft breeze blowing?

— a dog barking?

— a gentle rain?

When you love the world you are in for a marvelous adventure of discovery.

To do this you must be ready to enjoy with all
your senses. You must see from your heart
colors, textures, details, changes, brightness
and darkness. Loving the world involves
really looking for beauty and pleasure in
whatever you do.

Experience these memories with all your senses right now:

— gazing at farm fields, spring flowers, green hills, the moon and the stars; smelling freshly cut grass and cinnamon buns in the oven; tasting cold spring water or juicy berries; hearing waves at the beach, a loon or a child laughing; feeling wet grass between your toes, snow flakes on your tongue, a rose petal, the softness of a new baby, the warm purr of a kitten.

These are important ways of feeling a loving connection with life. You can feel this connection at any time in any place.

What are some of your favorite ways of
experiencing life? When did you last enjoy
them? What are some new ways you would
like to experience life?

Learning to love life also involves appreciation and respect. A respect for life comes from understanding that all living things depend on each other.

When you understand this relationship you
can experience curiosity, wonder, awe and
joy, calm and gentleness and a deeper
acceptance of everything that lives.

Loving life means being thankful for the opportunity to be alive, even when things go wrong — to breathe the air, to eat and sleep.

It means wanting to spread love to many people and places.

It means wanting to make the world a better place because you have lived.

PART 8

On Growing

Yes, you are growing. You have just grown,
through the pages of this book.

One caution: don't try to keep up with other people's growth or with their expectations of your growth.

Don't compare yourself with others or compete with them.

If a rose tried to grow like an oak tree it would sadly die trying. If an oak tree tried to smell like a rose it would sadly die trying. Take your growth steps one at a time — at your very own pace. 135

YOU ARE JUST RIGHT. You are growing beautifully in your own special way.

You are learning to live. You are learning to love.

Dear Reader,

If you have enjoyed this book, I hope you will share it with others.

As you have thoughts, feelings and ideas or experiences with loving, I would very much like to hear from you.

For now, I wish you much love and many rich blessings in living, moment by moment.

With Love,

Joanne Haynes-Klassen
c/o Jalmar Press
45 Hitching Post Drive, Building 23P
Rolling Hills Estates, California 90274

ABOUT THE AUTHOR

Joanne Haynes-Klassen wrote this book at 3 am on a bleak March morning. Her response to an inner calling to put these thoughts down on paper surprised her — she had never intended to write a book! Joanne enjoys staying in tune with what seems right from within, even though it may not seem a rational thing to do. Another book is now underway.

Joanne loves falling in love — with life, over and over again. She is very fond of campfires, ocean walks, bear hugs and belly laughs, organic gardening, babies and kids of all ages, small town bakeries, success stories and learning what's around the next corner.

ABOUT THE ARTISTS

Willene Moffatt-Cox

Willene's background spans a wide range of activities in the creative arts. Through painting, pottery, teaching, dancing and most recently a strong commitment to weaving, she has woven her way through life. Willene believes that a rich tapestry of expression can be created when message, theme and media are combined.

Willene's weavings are highly prized in private collections, public and office buildings across Canada. She lives with her daughter in Winnipeg, Manitoba, Canada.

Judy Ferguson

Judy Ferguson has had a wide range of creative experience in the professional art world. In addition to a strong background in design, she has a long list of credits as an illustrator which include the fashion and furniture industries and a major production company. Combining her experience in graphic design with illustrative skills, she has worked for several newspaper, magazine and book publications.

Judy lives with her daughter in Southern California. She loves birds and trees, flowers and cats, the ocean, mountains and friends — all of which she is currently involved in painting.

THIS OFFICIALLY CERTIFIES that the bearer is a **Very Important Person.** This **V.I.P.** is entitled to all the rights and privileges of a full-fledged member of the human race.

This **V.I.P.** is also bound by the responsibilities of this distinction: self care and integrity, responsiveness to others and a contribution to and respect for life.

Please treat this person with respect and you will receive the same.

ISSUED BY THE
LEARNING TO LIVE, LEARNING TO
LOVE SOCIETY

Jalmar Press

Officers: _____

Bradley L. Winch

_____
Joanne Haynes-Klassen

THE CREATIVE PARENTING/ CREATIVE TEACHING SERIES FROM JALMAR PRESS

The Creative Parenting/Creative Teaching Series presents an array of practical purposeful materials to help you in your job as a parent or other caring adult working with children. Parents are playing an increasingly vital role in their children's educations; teachers look for ways to effectively incorporate and assist parents' efforts at home as well as at school. Counselors, health practitioners, and educational specialists, too, look for useful materials that help them relate better to families and children.

Jalmar's Creative Parenting/Creative Teaching Series provides the support materials for all adult endeavors to enhance children's lives in meaningful and creative ways.

READING, WRITING, AND RAGE
The Terrible Price Paid by Victims of School Failure
by Dorothy Fink Ungerleider

An autopsy of one profound school failure, disclosing the complex processes behind it and the secret rage that grew out of it. It is time for the public to understand one of the most overlooked sources of rage in society.

$8.95 Paperback — 244 Pages

LEARNING TO LIVE, LEARNING TO LOVE
by Joanne Haynes-Klassen

An inspirational message for all ages about the importance of love in every thing we do. Beautifully told through words and pictures, **Learning to Live, Learning to Love** describes the human journey toward openness, forgiveness, and fulfillment.

$7.95   Illustrated Trade Paperback — 150 pages

FEELINGS ALPHABET
by Judy Lalli

Ever feel "ticklish," "wishy-washy" or "zonked"? These are a few of the feelings shown so effectively in this unique alphabet book which combines real-life photos with fascinating word graphics to convey the emotions of young children. By listening to and talking about the book, children will learn to express and accept their feelings.

$5.95   Black/White Photos — 72 Pages

THE CREATIVE PARENTING/ CREATIVE TEACHING SERIES FROM JALMAR PRESS (Continued)

UNICORNS ARE REAL: A Right-Brained Approach to Learning
by Barbara Meister Vitale

An illustrated activity book showing parents and teachers how to tap into children's "right-brained" strengths (using color, imagery, touch, sound, and movement) to teach "left-brain" school tasks.

$9.95   Trade Paperback — 118 Pages

CHARLES THE CLOWN'S GUIDE TO CHILDREN'S PARTIES
by Charles and Linda Kraus

A resource book of helpful party guidelines plus age-appropriate activities that naturally motivate and absorb children. Helps you to learn about all children as well as plan for that special event!

$9.95   Illustrated Trade Paperback — 304 Pages

"HE HIT ME BACK FIRST!" Creative Visualization Activities for Teaching & Parenting
by Eva D. Fugitt

Based on psychosynthesis, this activity book lovingly guides children to self-correcting behavior. Children become aware of choice and their "Wise Part Within" which helps them choose appropriate behaviors in all their interactions.

$9.95   Trade Paperback — 116 Pages

PITCHING IN: How to Teach Your Children to Work Around the House
by Charles Spellmann and Rachel Williams

Adults who worked around the house as children are more successful later in life, research shows. Here's a simple system plus sound parenting advice and humor, too!

$5.45   Illustrated Trade Paperback — 102 Pages

THE CREATIVE PARENTING /CREATIVE TEACHING SERIES FROM JALMAR PRESS (Concluded)

THE PARENT BOOK: The Holistic Program for Raising the Emotionally Mature Child by Harold Bessell and Thomas P. Kelly Jr.

A child-raising guide for children ages 3-14 that tells you how to live with your children in a way that encourages their healthy emotional development.

$9.95   Illustrated Trade Paperback — 204 Pages

WHOSE CHILD CRIES Children of Gay Parents Talk About Their Lives by Joe Gantz

This sensitive study presents the experiences of children in five families as they come to terms with their parent's lifestyles. Their straightforward and heartfelt explanations of what it is like growing up in their homes help make this book a valuable resource and excellent counseling tool. Foreword by Eda LeShan columnist for Women's Day Magazine.
$16.985   Hardbound $8.95 Softcover — 260 — Pages

PAJAMAS DON'T MATTER (OR: What Your Baby Really Needs) by Trish Gribben

Valuable information and needed reassurances to new parents as they struggle through the frantic, but rewarding, first years of their child's life.

$5.95   Illustrated Trade Paperback — 52 Pages

Write to Jalmar Press for free catalog describing these and other parenting/teaching materials for the handicapped and the gifted, as well as our full line of TA and Warm Fuzzy products for all ages.

JALMAR PRESS
45 Hitching Post Drive Building 2
Rolling Hills Estates, California 90274